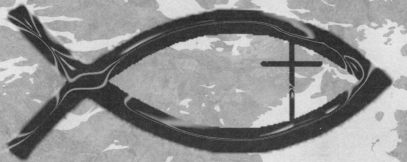

The Unabridged
Gospel

By Jerry W. Scheidbach

Distinctively Baptist
P U B L I C A T I O N S
Lighthouse Baptist Church
805.714.0786 • baptistlighthouse.org

Copyright © 2017 by Jerry Scheidbach

The Unabridged Gospel

By Jerry Scheidbach

Printed in the United States of America

ISBN: 9780982211007

All Bible quotations are taken from the Authorized King James Bible (KJB)

Peer Reviewed by Pastor Marshal Stevens, Pastor Max Graves, Pastor Jerry Cook, Pastor Brandon Campbell, Pastor Larry Cox, Evangelist David Mc-Cracken, and Evangelist Paul Abbott.

Dr. Jerry Scheidbach pastors the Lighthouse Baptist Church in Santa Maria, CA and hosts the radio broadcast/podcast show called "The Brain Massage"®. You can contact him by calling 805.714.0786 to reach his secretary, or send him an email to jscheidbach@me.com. You can hear "The Brain Massage"® show Online at www.santamarialighthouse.org, or brainmassage.net. For other books he has authored, go Online to booksatdbp.com.

Table of Contents

Quick Guide to Answers to Common Questions: After each question you will find direction to the page and paragraph where you can find the answer. For example, 9:1 means page 9 first paragraph, or part of a paragraph, on the page. Titles are not counted.

1. Meaning of the word gospel: 7:1; 12:1; 20:2

2. Can we be sure we'll go to Heaven? 8:5-9:4

3. Why did Jesus die and rise again? 12:2-22; 30:4-31:1

4. What does it mean to be lost? 12:3 - 16:3

5. Where did Lucifer, or Satan, come from? 12:3-15:1

6. Why did God give free will to mankind? 13:2-14:1

7. Why did man become sinful when he ate the fruit of the tree of the knowledge of good and evil? 14:3

8. If the wages for sin is death, why didn't Adam and Eve die immediately when they sinned? 14:3-15:1

9. Why do we go to hell for committing sins? 15:1-16:2

10. Why does Satan hate mankind so much? 12:3-13:1

11. Why did God allow Satan to tempt Adam and Eve? 13:2-14:1

12. Why did God allow all mankind to be condemned for the sin of Adam? 16:1; 17:2

13. Why does God refuse to allow even one sin into Heaven? 16:2

14. How can Jesus be the begotten Son of God? How can God have a Son? 17:3-18:1

15. How is it that the blood of Jesus pays for our sins and washes our sins away? 18:2-20:1

16. What does it mean to believe the gospel? 21:1

17. What does it mean to receive Jesus? 21:2

18. What does it mean to repent? 25:2-28:2; 29:2-30:1

19. What are the sins we must repent of? 26:1-28:2

20. How many sins must we commit before we are damned to hell fire? 28:3

21. Why do I sometimes feel guilty, and ashamed? 28:4-31:1

22. What happens if I refuse to repent and believe on Jesus? 30:2

23. What does the word remission mean? 30:3

24. How do I receive the remission Christ paid for my sins? 31:2-33:4

25. What, exactly, must I do to be saved and know it? 33:5-35:6

26. What must I do after I pray to receive Jesus as my Lord and Saviour? 36:1-4

27. How can I find a good church to help me learn the Bible? 37

~

The *Unabridged* Gospel

Preface

IXOYE—What do these letters mean? And what's with the symbol of a fish with the cross? What do I mean by The *Unabridged* Gospel, and why does it matter?

Let's start with why it matters. I'm concerned about the "many" Jesus said are deceived into thinking they have eternal life when they don't (Matthew 7:21-23). I'm also concerned about the many who do believe but they live with uncertainty about this important question (I John 5:13). And I'm concerned about those who are careless about spiritual things who will be horribly surprised when they die and end up in the fires of Hell. It matters because Jesus said if you die in your sins you cannot enter into Heaven, and you will be cast off into the Lake of Fire with the Devil and his angels (Revelation 20:11-15; Matthew 25:41).

The letters IXOYE stand for *Jesus Christ, God's Son, Saviour*. It comes from the Greek word for fish. When Christians were hunted down and killed in

Rome, the way they are today in Syria, and Iraq, by ISIS, Christians needed a secret way to identify one another. The Greek word for fish (ἰχθύς) served as an acronym standing for *Jesus Christ, God's Son, Saviour*. For this reason, believers used the fish as a symbol to identify a Christian. When they met as strangers, one could scribble an arc in the dirt, and the other could then complete the picture by drawing the second arc forming the outline of a fish. In this way, strangers could identify one another as Christians without giving themselves away to their persecutors.

The cross became a universally recognized symbol of Christianity as early as the second and third century. The purpose of using a cross to represent Christianity has the exact opposite motivation from the use of the fish as a symbol. The fish was used to provide a secret way to identify as a Christian, the cross was used as an open identification with Christianity.

I certainly do not fault Christians who used the fish to hide their identity; but if you think about it, the fish was a way of hiding the gospel too. Today, many facts about the gospel are as mysterious to many men and women as the secret meaning of the fish was to Romans long ago. How can "the blood" wash my sins away? How can a man be "born" when he is old? Why did God allow sin in the first place? What does it mean to repent? Why did God create Hell? There are biblical answers to these questions, but they seem to be secrets that are kept between the Christians. Combining the fish with the cross to me represents the idea of making the secrets of the gospel plain and open to everyone, the whole truth, the unabridged gospel.

What is the gospel? The word *gospel* means good news. It is the word used in the Bible to identify the good news that Jesus Christ, God's Son, died on the Cross for our sins, that He was buried, and on the third day He arose from the dead (I Corinthians 15:1-3). The reason this is good news is that if He had not died on the Cross for our sins and risen from the dead we could not have our sins forgiven, and, therefore, we could have no hope of eternal life. I'll explain this more in a moment. But this should be enough so you can know what we mean by the word *gospel*.

What do I mean by the unabridged gospel?

You have probably received or seen many gospel tracts—small pamphlets, or brochures, presenting the gospel. These are usually abbreviated versions of the gospel, where only the essential elements are culled out of Scripture and presented in a brief, concise fashion. The most famous is called *The Romans Road Map to Heaven*. There is nothing wrong with doing this. However, many times important questions are left unanswered, and even important truths are skipped over without adequate explanation.

I'll never forget it! I pulled into a gas station, got out of my car and walked around to the pump, and noticed the attendant was approaching me. For some reason, without thinking about it, I reached out my hand and greeted him. He was surprised, and took my hand, and told me his name. I looked at him and asked a simple question: "If you were to die today, are you 100% sure you would go to Heaven?"

He was stunned. Trembling, he reached into his shirt pocket and pulled out a little tract titled *The Romans*

Road Map To Heaven, and under the title, this question: "If you died today, are you 100% sure you would go to Heaven?" He told me he had been given the tract earlier that day, and was reading it, and was wondering whether in fact he would go to Heaven if he died. I explained some of the things he did not understand in the tract, and in a little while, that dear man bowed his head and sincerely prayed to receive Jesus Christ as his Lord and Saviour.

That little tract planted the seed, and God used it to waken his conscience and get him to thinking about where he would spend eternity. But in his case, he needed someone to help him understand what was not explained in the tract. Sometimes what is needed is an unabridged version of the gospel. That's what you have in your hands right now.

Everyone should read *The Unabridged Gospel*.

Jesus was concerned that many who believe they will spend eternity with Him in Heaven are deceived. He said, "Many will say unto me in that day, Lord, Lord, have we not prophesied in thy name? and in thy name have cast out devils? and in thy name done many wonderful works?" But Jesus is going to say to them, "I never knew you: depart from me, ye that work iniquity" (Matthew 7:22-23). How can this happen? How is it possible for someone to be so utterly deceived?

In the Bible God tells us to "make your calling and election sure" (II Peter 1:10). And we can be sure! The Bible says in I John 5:13, "These things have I written unto you that believe on the name of the Son of God, that ye may know that ye have eternal life."

Did you notice that this promise is addressed to those who "believe on the name of the Son of God"? Many believe in God, they believe in Jesus Christ, and yet they do not know for sure, with perfect peace and assurance, that they will go to Heaven when they die. God wants you to know that you have eternal life.

I'm concerned about the "many" Jesus said are deceived into thinking they have eternal life when they don't. I'm also concerned about the many who do believe, but live with uncertainty about this important question. And I'm concerned about those who are careless about spiritual things, heedless of the danger that "it is appointed unto man once to die, but after this the judgment" (Hebrews 9:27).

I've written *The Unabridged Gospel* to help anyone know for sure that they have eternal life.

~

The *Unabridged* Gospel

The Gospel Explained

Why did Jesus have to die for our sins so that we could be forgiven? Why do Christians talk about the need to be "saved"? What are we saved from? Christians talk about people being *lost;* what does that mean? And what about this business of the blood of Jesus washing away our sins? How can blood wash sins away? And what is *sin* anyway? Is God so cruel that He will burn someone in Hell forever simply because they break one of His rules? And why did God create man in such a way that he could sin if He did not want man to do that? The whole Christian gospel thing is confusing, even bewildering, to many people. *The Unabridged Gospel* answers all of these questions and more.

Along with the answers and explanations that you'll find in the following pages, you'll see numbers at key places that correspond to a Scripture reference printed in a box along side the text. Please read these Scriptures along with the text.

Jesus told His disciples to go into all the world and preach the gospel to every creature (Mark 16:15). The gospel is the good news that, according to the Scriptures (the Bible), Jesus died for our sins, was buried, and rose again the third day (I Corinthians 15:1-3).

Why did Jesus die and then rise from the dead?

According to the Scriptures, He did this in order to seek and save the lost (Luke 19:10; John 10:15-17).

> "For the Son of man is come to seek and to save that which was lost."
> Luke 19:10

The Story of How Mankind Was "Lost" to God.

God's most powerful Angel, Lucifer (a.k.a. Satan), was perfect in wisdom and beauty until iniquity (unrighteousness) was found in him ([1] Ezekiel 28:13-19). Although God gave him great riches, glory, and power, he began to envy God's greater riches, glory, and power. The first lie was birthed in Lucifer's heart ([1a] John 8:44). He deceived himself into believing that he would exalt his throne above the stars of God and be "like the Most High" ([2] Isaiah 14:12-17). He deceived 1/3 of the heavenly host into joining him in his rebellion ([3] Revelation 12:4; see 1:20). God took dust of the earth, and formed a

1. Ezekiel 28:15 "Thou wast perfect in thy ways from the day that thou wast created, till iniquity was found in thee."

1a John 8:44 "…he (the Devil) is a liar and the father of it."

2. Isaiah 14:14 "I will ascend above the heights of the clouds; I will be like the most High."

3. Revelation 12:4 "And his tail drew the third part of the stars of heaven, and did cast them to the earth …" (Stars are used to represent angels in Revelation 1:20.)

creature inferior to the angels, called man, and from the man He made the woman, and gave to them what Lucifer coveted (lusted for)—the image and likeness of God ([4] Genesis 1:26,27).

Their names were Adam and Eve and they lived in a garden called Eden, and Lucifer hated them (Genesis 1-3; Revelation 12:9).

> 4. Genesis 1:27 "So God created man in his own image, in the image of God created he him; male and female created he them."

God loved Adam and Eve. He desired them to do what gratefulness and conscience would require—to love Him in return ([5] Matthew 22:37; see I John 4:8). God cannot lie ([6] Titus 1:2), and would not pretend they loved Him unless they were free to choose. God showed His love by granting to them the gift of free will. In this way, they could, in their turn, show their love for Him by yielding their will to His in obedience ([7] John 14:15; Genesis 2:17). He warned them that the consequence of disobedience would be death (Genesis 2:17; [8] Romans 6:23).

> 5. Matthew 22:37 "Jesus said unto him, Thou shalt love the Lord thy God with all thy heart, and with all thy soul, and with all thy mind."
>
> 6. Titus 1:2 "... God, that cannot lie, ..."
>
> 7. John 14:15 "If ye love me, keep my commandments."
>
> 8. Romans 6:23 "For the wages of sin is death ..."

Making man in God's image did not mean God gave to man all of God's attributes (characteristics). For example, God did not make man omnipotent (all powerful) or omniscient (all knowing). However, one of the characteristics of God that He did not immediately give to man was the knowledge of good and evil.

God placed the tree of the knowledge of good and evil in the garden, within the reach of man, and commanded them not to eat of its fruit. Remembering the backdrop to this is Lucifer's own evil coveting of God's image and likeness, we can appreciate the appropriateness of this test of man's love. Adam and Eve would soon show whether or not they would follow Lucifer's example, who coveted God's likeness, and trespass against God's law (which is sin) to get it.

Lucifer entered into the Garden and lied to Eve ([9] John 8:44). He told her that God prohibited her from eating of that fruit because He did not want her to be "as God, knowing good and evil." Also, he told her that she would not surely die if she ate of the fruit. Eve believed Satan's lie ([10] I Timothy 2:14). After she ate, she offered the fruit to her husband and he joined her in disobedience (sin) against God.

9. John 8:44 "... the devil, ... is a liar, and the father of it."

10. 1Timothy 2:14 "And Adam was not deceived, but the woman being deceived was in the transgression."

Adam and Eve ate the fruit in disobedience to God, perhaps that is why the evil aspect of the knowledge of good and evil dominated their nature. Thus corrupted, they opened the door to death ([11] Romans 5:12,13).

Death occurs physically when our soul (life) is separated from our body ([12] Genesis 35:18).

11. Romans 5:12 "Wherefore, as by one man sin entered into the world, and death by sin; and so death passed upon all men, for that all have sinned ..."

12. Genesis 35:18 "And it came to pass, as her soul was in departing, (for she died) ..."

Death occurs spiritually when our spirit is separated from our God ([13] Ephesians 2:1; Isaiah 59:2). Immediately, they died spiritually. And physically they began down that slow and agonizing path of aging that ends in the grave.

But more devastating was the fact that the nature of man was corrupted by his sin. This corrupted nature, and its evil fruit, death, was passed on to all Adam's descendants through his seed ([See 11] Romans 5:12). Sin and death now reside in the body of all born of Adam who are therefore under the power of sin ([14] Acts 26:18), which spiritually makes them children of Lucifer (a.k.a. the Serpent, Satan, or the Devil [15] I John 3:10; Revelation 12:9).

13. Ephesians 2:1 "And you hath he quickened, who were dead in trespasses and sins ..."

14. Acts 26:18 "To ... turn them ... from the power of Satan unto God, ..."

15. 1John 3:10 "In this the children of God are manifest, and the children of the devil: whosoever doeth not righteousness is not of God, ..."

16. Matthew 25:41 "Then shall he say also unto them on the left hand, Depart from me, ye cursed, into everlasting fire, prepared for the devil and his angels ..."

For this reason, all who die in their sins will face the same judgment prepared for Satan and his angels — to be cast alive into the lake of fire that burns with fire and brimstone for eternity ([16] Matthew 25:41; Revelation 14:10; 20:10-15; 21:8).

Perhaps you think it is unfair for God to allow the penalty of death to pass on to all Adam's descendants. But we are reminded of this truth daily. For example, the addicted mother passes her addiction to the child in her womb. When this happens, it's not the fault of the child; but the relationship between the mother and child is one that the behavior of the sinful mother has a direct impact upon the innocent child. When Adam sinned, the damage it caused was passed on to us. That damage was sin and death.

We must remember that God did not create sin in man, and it was not His desire that man would sin. He did not willingly subject His creature to this vanity, but did it in hope ([17] Romans 8:20).

Now consider the wisdom and mercy of God. Because the sin of one man brought sin and death into the world, God may justly deliver all from sin and death by the righteousness of one man ([18] Romans 5:13-18).

That man might know the truth about sin, God, Who cannot lie, must allow its consequence to be seen. And the ravages of sin that we see justifies God setting upon it the limit of death. Therefore, God has decreed that all who die in their sins must go to Hell, where sin can never again hurt the innocent ([19] Hebrews 9:27; [20] II Thessalonians 1:8).

17. Romans 8:20 "For the creature was made subject to vanity, not willingly, but by reason of him who hath subjected the same in hope."

18. Romans 5:18, (19) "Therefore as by the offence of one judgment came upon all men to condemnation; even so by the righteousness of one the free gift came upon all men unto justification of life."

19. Hebrews 9:27 "And as it is appointed unto men once to die, but after this the judgment ..."

20. II Thessalonians 1:8 "In flaming fire taking vengeance on them that know not God, and that obey not the gospel of our Lord Jesus Christ ..."

Now that you know how mankind was lost to God, and why we need a Saviour, the next question is how did God arrange to bring salvation to mankind?

The Story of How God Brought Salvation to Mankind.

There is nothing man can do to make up for his sins, or to remove them from before God. The Bible says our righteousness is no better than filthy rags ([21] Isaiah 64:6; Titus 3:5). In this case, how can anyone be saved? Jesus said that with men this is impossible; but with God, all things are possible ([22] Matthew 19:24-26).

21. Isaiah 64:6 "But we are all as an unclean thing, and all our righteousnesses are as filthy rags; and we all do fade as a leaf; and our iniquities, like the wind, have taken us away."

The Bible says that if all are made sinners by one man's sin, then by the righteousness of one, all may be made righteous ([See 18 on page 16] Romans 5:18,19). If somehow we could be born again from a sinless "Adam," we would then have a sinless nature. The good news is that God made it possible for us to be born again of a sinless "Adam."

22. Matthew 19:25-26 "... his disciples (said), Who then can be saved? ... Jesus ... said unto them, With men this is impossible; but with God all things are possible."

23. Hebrews 1:3 "Who being the brightness of his glory, and the express image of his person ..."

24. Philippians 2:5-6 "Let this mind be in you, which was also in Christ Jesus: Who, being in the form of God, thought it not robbery to be equal with God ..."

God sent Christ (means the Anointed one) into the world to save sinners. According to the Bible, Christ is the eternal image of the invisible God, the express image of His Person (Colossians 1:15; [23] Hebrews 1:3). He was in the "form" of God before He became a man ([24] Philippians 2:6)

In a manner of speaking, Christ is to God what our body is to us ([25] I Thessalonians 5:23). As He is the expression of God, He is also called the "Word" ([26] John 1:1,14). And the "Word" is called God's Seed ([27] I Peter 1:23; see also Galatians 3:16). God joined His Seed with the seed of a woman named Mary. The child thus conceived was both the Son of Man, and the Son of God (John 1:1,14; Philippians 2:5-11).

God, by joining His Seed (the Word) with the woman's seed, bypassed the corruption that was in Adam (John 1:1,14). This produced a new sinless man, the only begotten Son of God, Whom the Bible says is, "God manifest in the flesh" ([28] I Timothy 3:16). The Bible refers to this new man as the "Last Adam" ([29] I Corinthians 15:45). God commanded that His Name would be *Jesus*, because He would save His people from their sins ([30] Matthew 1:21). Here is how.

Because He was the Son of Man, He could die on man's

25. I Thessalonians 5:23 "... your whole spirit and soul and body ..."

26. John 1:1,14 "In the beginning was the Word, and the Word was with God, and the Word was God. ... And the Word was made flesh, and dwelt among us, (and we beheld his glory, the glory as of the only begotten of the Father,) full of grace and truth."

27. I Peter 1:23 "Being born again, not of corruptible seed, but of incorruptible, by the word of God, which liveth and abideth for ever."

28. I Timothy 3:16 "... God was manifest in the flesh ..."

29. I Corinthians 15:45 "The first man Adam was made a living soul; the last Adam was made a quickening spirit."

30. Matthew 1:21 "thou shalt call his name JESUS: for he shall save his people from their sins."

behalf, thus paying the wages of sin ([31]Romans 6:23; 5:8).

Yet, since He was the Son of God, He was sinless, which means the life (soul) in His blood ([32]Leviticus 17:11) was without sin. For this reason, His soul did not have to go into hell fire after He died. Instead, His soul could reclaim his body from death and rise from the grave ([33]John 10:17).

The wages of sin is death. God sent His Son to die in our place. He accepted the death of Jesus on the cross as payment in full for our sins. And He decreed that all who receive Jesus are washed from their sins by His sinless blood ([34]Revelation 1:5; Ephesians 1:7; Hebrews 9:12). How?

According to the Bible, our life (or *soul*) is in the blood (Leviticus 17:11). The soul that sins shall die ([35]Ezekiel 18:20). Our blood is polluted. When we believe on Jesus, we believe to the saving of our soul ([36]Hebrews 10:39). Our *life* is washed from our sins by Christ's sinless blood. His *life* is then put into our heart by His Spirit, and that is the *life* we now live in the flesh ([37]Galatians 2:20).

31. Romans 6:23 "For the wages of sin is death… ."

32. Leviticus 17:11 "For the life of the flesh is in the blood …"

33. John 10:17 "Therefore doth my Father love me, because I lay down my life, that I might take it again."

34. Revelation 1:5 "And from Jesus Christ, who … loved us, and washed us from our sins in his own blood …"

35. Ezekiel 18:20 "The soul that sinneth, it shall die."

36. Hebrews 10:39 "… believe to the saving of the soul."

37. Galatians 2:20 "I am crucified with Christ: nevertheless I live; yet not I, but Christ liveth in me: and the life which I now live in the flesh I live by the faith of the Son of God, who loved me, and gave himself for me."

God has decreed that all who receive His Son will be given the power to become a child of God ([38] John 1:11-13). How does that happen?

When we receive Jesus Christ, the Spirit of God removes us from Adam and places us into Christ (I Corinthians 12:13; [39] Galatians 3:27). As in Adam we inherited death, so now in Christ we inherit the free gift of everlasting life ([40]John 10:28; I John 5:12-13). The life we receive from Jesus is sinless, and eternal, so all who receive this life are eternally saved from hell fire (John 1:11-13; Hebrews 10:39; [41]Romans 5:9).

The gospel is the good news that Jesus Christ has died for our sins, according to the Scriptures, and that He was buried and arose again the third day according to the Scriptures, and that all who believe the gospel will be saved ([42] I Corinthians 15:1-3).

38. John 1:11-13 "... But as many as received him, to them gave he power to become the sons of God ..."

39. Galatians 3:27 "For as many of you as have been baptized into Christ have put on Christ."

40. John 10:28 "And I give unto them eternal life; and they shall never perish ...."

41. Romans 5:9 "we shall be saved from wrath through him ..."

42. I Corinthians 15:1-3 "Moreover, brethren, I declare unto you the gospel which I preached unto you, which also ye have received, and wherein ye stand; by which also ye are saved, if ye keep in memory what I preached unto you, unless ye have believed in vain. For I delivered unto you first of all that which I also received, how that Christ died for our sins according to the scriptures; and that he was buried, and that he rose again the third day according to the scriptures ..."

But what exactly does it mean to *believe* the gospel?

What does it mean to believe the gospel?

Believing on Jesus means you are trusting in Him, and in Him alone, to save you ([43] Proverbs 3:5). He said, "I am the way, the truth and the life. No man cometh unto the Father but by Me" (John 14:6). You must not trust in any church to save you – Baptist, Protestant, Catholic, cult, or any other religion. Nor should you trust in any baptism, or in your own good works. You must trust in the Lord Jesus alone as your only hope for salvation.

If you trust Him, then you will draw near to Him, and receive Him ([44] Hebrews 10:22; [45] John 1:11-13). And to receive Him means you confess He is your Lord and Master. It means you accept Him as your only hope to be saved from God's wrath.

43. Proverbs 3:5 "Trust in the LORD with all thine heart … ."

44. Hebrews 10:22 "Let us draw near with a true heart in full assurance of faith …"

45. John 1:12 "But as many as received him, to them gave he power to become the sons of God…"

46. Revelation 1:5 "Unto him that loved us, and washed us from our sins in his own blood …"

47. I Peter 1:23 "Being born again, … by the word of God, …"

48. Galatians 4:6 "And because ye are sons, God hath sent forth the Spirit of his Son into your hearts, crying, Abba, Father."

Receiving Jesus means believing your sins are washed away by the blood He shed on Calvary ([46] Revelation 1:5). The moment that you, by faith, receive Jesus Christ, you are birthed to God by the Word of His Spirit (John 1:11-13; [47] I Peter 1:23). At the very moment that you repent of your sins and call on Him in prayer to save you, God will make you one of His children (John 1:12; [48] Galatians 4:6).

The critical point here is that belieivng the gospel means believing on the name of our Lord Jesus Christ. What does this mean?

Scripture tells us there is "no other name under heaven given among men, whereby we must be saved" (Acts 4:12). *Jesus* is that name. Everything that makes up a person is invested in their name. That's why "a good name is rather to be chosen than great riches" (Proverbs22:1). A name identifies and describes.

The name *Jesus* is made up of two Hebrew words that together mean Jehovah saves. Jehovah is God's name. It's like saying, "God our Saviour"—and this expression is used six times in the Bible (I Timothy 1:1; 2:3; Titus 1:3; 2:10; 3:4; and Jude 25). The name *Jesus,* therefore, identies Christ as *God our Saviour.*

He is the eternal Word, who in the beginning was with God, and was God—John 1:1 "In the beginning was the word, and the word was with God, and the word was God." He is the word made flesh (John 1:14), so that He is "God manifest in the flesh" (I Timothy 3:16). He is the creator of all things (Colossians 1:16— "For by him [Jesus] were all things created.") And as the Son of God, He died on the cross to pay the wages for our sins.

The connection between receiving Jesus as Saviour and believing on His name is made clear in John 1:12, "But as many as received Him, to them gave He power to become the sons of God, even unto them that believe on His name."

To believe "on His name" you must accept what the Bible says about Jesus.

~

The *Unabridged* Gospel

"What Must I Do To Be Saved?"
How to be 100% certain you have eternal life!

An earthquake shook the prison doors opened, but every prisoner remained in their cell. Paul, the great Christian Missionary, and his partner, Silas, were among them and had been praying and singing praises to God when the earthquake hit. The jailer came trembling, and, kneeling before them, cried out, "Sirs, what must I do to be saved?" (Acts 16:30). That's the question I answer in this chapter. What exactly must you do to be saved?

You have learned why you need to be saved, and what that means, but what should you do with this information? Paul gave the answer, "Believe on the Lord Jesus Christ, and thou shalt be saved" (Acts 16:31). Is that it? Is it true that if you "believe on the Lord Jesus" you are saved?

The next verse, Acts 16:32, tells us that Paul explained further what it means to "believe on the Lord Jesus Christ." In this chapter I explain what it means to "believe on the Lord Jesus Christ."

Repentance and Remission of Sins

Jesus instructed His followers to preach this gospel message (see above) to every person in the world, in every generation ([49] Mark 16:15). But we must do it the way He told us to do it. He told us to preach repentance and remission of sins ([50] Luke 24:46-47) – not repentance only, or remission only. Here is the reason almost 80% of Americans claim to be "born again," and yet as a nation we are on a collision course with the wrath of God for our many sins.

Satan blinds the minds of the lost so that they will not be saved (see [51] II Corinthians 4:4). He has deceived many churches so that they either preach repentance without remission, or remission without repentance. Therefore, churches are filled with persons who cry, "Lord, Lord," but do not do what Jesus says ([52] Luke 6:46).

49. Mark 16:15 "And he said unto them, Go ye into all the world, and preach the gospel to every creature."

50. Luke 24:46,47 "And said unto them, ... that repentance and remission of sins should be preached in his name among all nations ..."

51. II Corinthians 4:4 "In whom the god of this world hath blinded the minds of them which believe not ...."

52. Luke 6:46 "And why call ye me, Lord, Lord, and do not the things which I say?"

Probably the primary reason churches have so little influence upon the conscience of our nation is because so many church members today are not truly saved. Jesus did say there would be many in that day who will be surprised to hear Him say, "I never knew you."

The churches must preach both repentance and remission of sins because there is no other way for men to be saved than to repent and receive Jesus for the remission (payment) of their sins. Therefore, please listen very carefully to the truth about repentance and remission of sins.

Repentance is God's command to all men everywhere to turn from sin and flee to Him for salvation from His judgment ([53] Acts 17:30; [54] 26:17-18). The word *remission* means payment. The wages of sin is death, and so to preach remission is to declare that God has received the death of His own Son as payment in full for all our sins. God has commanded us to believe this truth about His Son, and to receive Him as our Lord and Savior.

Therefore, to preach the gospel means we declare the good news that God so loved the world, He gave His only begotten Son, that whosoever believeth in Him should not perish, but have everlasting life ([55] John 3:16). And we call on all men to repent, and to believe the Gospel (Mark 1:15).

53. Acts 17:30 "... God ... now commandeth all men every where to repent ..."

54. Acts 26:18 "To open their eyes, and to turn them from darkness to light, and from the power of Satan unto God, that they may receive forgiveness of sins, and inheritance among them which are sanctified by faith that is in me."

55. John 3:16 "For God so loved the world, that he gave his only begotten Son, that whosoever believeth in him should not perish, but have everlasting life."

What must you do to be saved?

<u>Repent of your sins.</u> Because you are a sinner, you have at times chosen to disobey God's law, which is what it means to sin. The sins that are common to men are listed in the Bible ([56] Galatians 5:19-21; Matthew 15:19).

The list begins with adultery, fornication, uncleanness (physical and moral impurity) and lasciviousness (means lustful).

Adultery occurs when someone who is married has sex with someone other than their spouse. Most people

> 56. Galatians 5:19-21
> "Now the works of the flesh are manifest, which are these; adultery, fornication, uncleanness, lasciviousness, idolatry, witchcraft, hatred, variance, emulations, wrath, strife, seditions, heresies, envyings, murders, drunkenness, revellings, and such like: of the which I tell you … they which do such things shall not inherit the kingdom of God."

think that **fornication** is having sex before marriage. But fornication (from the Greek *pornoeo*) also includes pornography, homosexuality, incest, bestiality, in short, all sexual deviancy. **Uncleanness** refers to physical and moral impurity. Bad hygiene encourages the spread of physical disease, and moral impurity includes any thought or action that spreads spiritual diseases that corrupt the conscience. **Lasciviousness** refers to behavior that is expressive of impure sexual desires. Sexual harassment, behavior that is expressive of, or intended to arouse, inappropriate sexual interest, or to entice someone into sinful sexual behavior, all are included in the sin of lasciviousness.

Jesus said that if we look on a woman to lust after her in our heart, we are guilty of adultery. Therefore, whether these things are done physically, or mentally, they are sinful ([57]Matthew 5:28).

The list continues with **idolatry** (the use of images in worship ([58]Exodus 20:4,5)), and **witchcraft** (Ouija Boards, Astrology, Horoscopes, Wicca, tarot cards, casting spells, palm reading, communicating with the dead). The Bible says that covetousness (lusting greedily for anything) is idolatry ([59]Colossians 3:5). And He warns us that involvement in any of these things brings us into contact with, and under the influence of devils ([60]I Corinthians 10:20).

Then God names **hatred**, variance (always arguing), **emulations** (striving to equal), **wrath** (outrageous anger), **strife**, and **sedition** (encouraging divisions between others). Jesus said if we hate a brother in our heart, we are guilty of murder ([61]I John 3:15). Who is your brother? All are born of Adam, and in that sense, all mankind are brothers. Bigotry, racial and religious discrimination, hating one another, all are sins against God Who created all of us in His image and likeness.

57. Matthew 5:28 "... whosoever looketh on a woman to lust after her hath committed adultery with her already in his heart."

58. Exodus 20:4,5 "Thou shalt not make unto thee any graven image ... thou shalt not bow down thyself to them, nor serve them ..."

59. Colossians 3:5 "... and covetousness, which is idolatry ..."

60. 1Corinthians 10:20 "But I say, that the things which the Gentiles sacrifice, they sacrifice to devils, and not to God: and I would not that ye should have fellowship with devils."

61. 1John 3:15 "Whosoever hateth his brother is a murderer: and ye know that no murderer hath eternal life abiding in him."

The list goes on to name **heresies** (false beliefs, false teaching), **envying**, **murders**, **drunkenness** (use of alcohol or drugs to compromise sobriety), and **reveling** (excessive partying, carousing).

In [62] Revelation 21:8 the Bible says that all **liars** will have their part in the lake of fire.

Remember that Adam and Eve only offended in one law of God and they were condemned as sinners. Even if you have offended in only one of the above sins you are condemned by God as a sinner and need to be saved. For God warns you that if you die in your sins, you will go into hell fire ([63] Hebrews 9:27). But He loves you, and has provided a way for you to be saved.

Even though you cannot see the Holy Spirit, He is at this very moment reproving your heart for your sins ([64] John 16:7-11). You should be experiencing a sense of guilt and shame, and a fear of judgment to come that you know you deserve. This is called conviction. It means you are responding appropriately to the Spirit's reproof upon your heart. If you are not experiencing conviction, it means your heart is hardened in sin, and

62. Revelation 21:8 "... and all liars, shall have their part in the lake which burneth with fire and brimstone: which is the second death."

63. Hebrews 9:27 "And as it is appointed unto men once to die, but after this the judgment ..."

64. John 16:7-11 "... And when he is come, he will reprove the world of sin, and of righteousness, and of judgment: of sin, because they believe not on me; of righteousness, because I go to my Father, and ye see me no more; of judgment, because the prince of this world is judged."

that you love the darkness of lies more than the light of truth. The reason you love darkness more than light is because you want to continue in your sins. You are wicked (rebellious against God), and damned to the eternal fires of hell because you love sin more than righteousness (⁶⁵ John 3:17-21). Be forewarned, you will be judged by God's righteousness, not your own (⁶⁶ Romans 10:3). Flee to God for mercy and ask Him to humble your heart, and to grant you repentance before it is too late (⁶⁷ II Timothy 2:25). If you are experiencing conviction it means God has granted to you repentance, and you would do well to receive it.

65. John 3:17-21 "... he that believeth not is condemned already, because he hath not believed in the name of the only begotten Son of God. And this is the condemnation, that light is come into the world, and men loved darkness rather than light, because their deeds were evil. For every one that doeth evil hateth the light, neither cometh to the light, lest his deeds should be reproved. But he that doeth truth cometh to the light, that his deeds may be made manifest, that they are wrought in God."

66. Romans 10:3 "For they being ignorant of God's righteousness, and going about to establish their own righteousness, have not submitted themselves unto the righteousness of God."

67. 2Timothy 2:25 "... if God peradventure will give them repentance to the acknowledging of the truth ..."

Okay, so, how do you repent?

God has commanded you to repent. This means you must turn from the power of Satan to God (turn to God to deliver you from the power of Satan) and from darkness to light (which is to turn away from your false beliefs to the truth) and then to *believe on* Jesus, which means to trust Him to save you ([68] Acts 26:18).

All who refuse to obey the gospel command to repent and believe on Jesus Christ will face the fiery wrath of God almighty ([69] II Thessalonians 1:8; Matthew 25:41). Embrace the wonderful love of God and be born into His family and be saved today. Here is how.

68. Acts 26:18 "To open their eyes, and to turn them from darkness to light, and from the power of Satan unto God, that they may receive forgiveness of sins, and inheritance among them which are sanctified by faith that is in me."

69. II Thessalonians 1:8 "In flaming fire taking vengeance on them that know not God, and that obey not the gospel of our Lord Jesus Christ ..."

Receive the remission of sins.

The word *remission* means the cancellation of a debt, or a penalty. The wages (payment) of sin is death ([70]Romans 6:23). We all have sinned, and so we all owe this debt. After we

70. For the wages of sin is death..."

die, we face the penalty of God's judgment (Hebrews 9:27). Jesus said His blood was shed for the remission of sins ([70] Matthew 26:28). His blood was accepted by the Father

71. "For this is my blood of the new testament, which is shed for many for the remission of sins."

as payment (remittance) which cancels our debt and our penalty for sin. Why does God accept the blood of His Son as remittance for our sins?

When Christ died, He died for us, that is, He took our place

72. "But God commendeth His love toward us, in that, while we were yet sinners, Christ died for us."

and died for our sins ([72]Romans 5:8). In this way the

payment for our sin was remitted (canceled), because it was paid in full when He shed His blood on the Cross. And so God accepts the blood of His Son as remittance (payment) for our sins.

How do we "receive the remission of sins"? God received the remittance that Jesus provided on our behalf for our sins. We had no way to pay our debt but to die and face the judgment of eternal damnation. But God loved us, and gave His Son Who shed His blood as remittance (payment to cancel a debt) for the wages we owed for our sins. When we talk about receiving the remission of sins we mean we must accept the truth that Jesus' death on the Cross paid it all.

We acknowledge that Jesus' death on the cross alone had the power to cancel the debt and the penalty of our sins. No amount of good works, or good deeds of any kind, can wipe one sin from our record or reduce our indebtedness to God for our sins. We are saved from the wages of sin and the penalty that follows "not by works of righteousness which we have done, but according to His mercy He saved us" (Titus 3:5). In His mercy, He provided payment in full for all our sins—He paid the remittance. Now, all we have to do is receive the remission.

In fact, to receive the remission of sins means to receive Jesus Himself— "as many as received Him to them gave He power to become the sons of God" (John 1:13). God received the remittance Jesus paid on our behalf, and we receive the remission of our sins when we accept Jesus as our Lord and Saviour, acknowledging that what He did for us on the Cross canceled our debt and penalty for sin.

How do I receive the remission of sins? We do this by faith—we believe God's promise, we accept His free gift.

Receiving the remission is the critical step. Many people repent, but they never surrender to God's righteousness for their salvation—they continue to hold on to the notion that their own good works, in the end, must be what God requires in order to save them. This is a mistake that makes the difference between Hell and Heaven.

We cannot be saved by our own good works. The Bible says, "For by grace are ye saved, through faith, and that not of yourselves, it is the gift of God, not of works, lest any man should boast" (Ephesians 2:8-9). Unless you humble yourself and submit to God's righteousness, and repent of the notion that your own righteousness will save you, you cannot be saved ([73] Romans 10:3).

I often use the following simple illustration to explain the difference between asking for salvation, and actually receiving it.

> 73. "For they being ignorant of God's righteousness, and going about to establish their own righteousness, have not submitted themselves unto the righteousness of God."

Imagine me offering to give you a gift. Remember, salvation is the "gift of God." If I purchased a gift and then offered it to you, when does it actually become yours? When you take it, of course. You do not have or possess the gift until you actually receive it.

Imagine me holding out a gift to you while you are asking me for it. You keep asking me for the gift, over and over again. And I continue holding the gift out to you, offering it to you; although you are asking for it, you will never have it until you take it. You can ask God for forgiveness and salvation a million times, but you will never have it until you receive it.

Many people are like that. They are repentant for their sins, and they ask for forgiveness, they even ask God to save them, and they do this repeatedly. But they are not saved, and they will never be saved until by faith they believe and receive the remission that God has provided for them.

The problem is that many simply refuse to believe that it's that easy. Of course, there is nothing easy about it, if you look at if from God's point of view. The suffering of His Son on the Cross was an ordeal that has impacted God for eternity. And, with regard to it being "too easy" for us, that is the wrong question. The question is how much would we have to do. The simple fact is that there is no amount of work any one could ever do that would wipe away one single sin from our record. The truth is that unless God did it all for us we would be damned and without hope.

It comes down to faith, not works. We must believe! It's our only way to be saved. God's gracious provision of forgiveness and salvation is extended to us as God's gift to sinful man. That gift becomes ours when we receive it by faith: "For by grace are ye saved, through faith" (Ephesians 2:8-9).

Okay, so what must you do, right now, in order to be saved and know it?

If you will obey God's command to repent and believe on Jesus Christ, here is what you need to do.

God has spelled it out for us in very simple terms. You will find it in [74] Romans 10:9.

> 74. "That if thou shalt confess with thy mouth the Lord Jesus, and shalt believe in thine heart that God hath raised Him from the dead, thou shalt be saved."

You must confess with your mouth the Lord Jesus ([74] Romans 10:9a). This means you confess that only Jesus is the Christ, the Son of God, which means He is your Master and your Lord ([75] II John 1:7-9; [76]John 13:13).

> 75. "For many deceivers are entered into the world, who confess not that Jesus Christ is come in the flesh. This is a deceiver and an antichrist."

You must believe that He arose from the grave according to the Scriptures ([77] I Corinthians 15:1-3). According to the Scriptures, Jesus arose physically — His body came out of the grave (Matthew 28:6; [78] Luke 24:39).

> 76. "Ye call me Master and Lord: and ye say well; for so I am."

> 77. "... And ... he rose again the third day according to the scriptures ..."

> 78. "Behold my hands and my feet, that it is I myself: handle me, and see; for a spirit hath not flesh and bones, as ye see me have."

Jesus said "Behold my hands and my feet…a spirit hath not flesh and bones, as ye see me have,"[(78)] to His disciples after He arose from the dead. Jesus wanted His disciples to know that He arose physically from the grave.

You must confess with your mouth that Jesus is Lord, and you must believe what the Bible says about His resurrection. However…

Confessing He is Lord and believing He arose is necessary to be saved, but this alone does not mean you are saved ([79] Matthew 7:22; James 2:19).

What next?

You need to pray.

The Bible says, "For whosoever shall call upon the name of the Lord, shall be saved" (Romans 10:13). To "call upon the name of the Lord" means to pray to God the Father in Jesus' Name ([80] John 14:13).

79. Matthew 7:22,23 "Many will say to me in that day, Lord, Lord, have we not prophesied in thy name? and in thy name have cast out devils? and in thy name done many wonderful works? And then will I profess unto them, I never knew you: depart from me, ye that work iniquity."

80. John 14:13 "And whatsoever ye shall ask in my name, that will I do, that the Father may be glorified in the Son."

When we pray, we ask God for what we want or need. To be saved you need forgiveness of your sins. To receive this forgiveness, you need to ask God for it ([81] James 4:1-2).

81. James 4:2 "...Ye have not because ye ask not..."

Find a quiet place to pray. Confess that Jesus is your Lord, and ask God to forgive your sins in Jesus' name. Then thank God in the Name of Jesus for saving your soul. For, according to the Scriptures, God cannot lie,[82] and He promised that if you do this, your sins are washed away ([83] Revelation 1:5).

82. Titus 1:2 "In hope of eternal life, which God, that cannot lie, promised before the world began."

83. "Unto Him that loved us, and washed us from our sins in His own blood."

If you have repented, turning to God, and received the remission of sins by faith in Jesus as your Lord and Saviour, Jesus has made you a child of God ([84] John 1:11-13). And He has given you the gift of eternal life ([85] John 10:28; Romans 6:23).

> 84. "He came unto his own, and his own received him not. But as many as received him, to them gave he power to become the sons of God, even to them that believe on his name: which were born, not of blood, nor of the will of the flesh, nor of the will of man, but of God."
>
> 85. "Unto Him that loved us, and washed us from our sins in His own blood."
>
> 85. "And I give unto them eternal life; and they shall never perish, neither shall any man pluck them out of my hand."

Jesus made it clear that those who refuse to confess Him before men will be denied by Him before the Father ([86] Matthew 10:32-33). If you prayed in Jesus' name to be saved, then you need to tell someone about it.

> 86. "Whosoever therefore shall confess me before men, him will I confess also before my Father ... But whosoever shall deny me before men, him will I also deny before my Father which is in Heaven."

Also, as a newborn in Christ, you need to feed on the sincere milk of God's word, which means you need to begin studying the Bible ([87] I Peter 2:2).

> 87. "As newborn babes, desire the sincere milk of the word, that ye may grow thereby."

We would be thrilled to hear from you. You will find our contact information on the back cover. We would be delighted to meet you and do all we can to help you grow in your knowledge of God's Word. You have friends at Lighthouse Baptist Church.

As a Christian, you can help influence the world toward Christ by learning to be a faithful servant of Almighty God. To learn how to serve God faithfully, and make a difference in your life, and in the lives of those you love, contact us.

Lighthouse Baptist Church *Invites You ...*

We are located at
1310 W. Betteravia Road
Santa Maria, CA 93455 (Call 805-714-0786)

We gather for public worship On Sundays

9:30 AM *Featuring*

Adult Bible Studies (Call for information about current classes)

Children's Ministry — Nursery through High School. We provide a program called Hero's of the Faith, developing a generation of heroes for Christ, one child at a time.

10:45 AM *Featuring* Light From the Helm - "Old Path" Bible preaching that tells it like it is, without fear or compromise.

5:00 PM *Featuring* Ministry Leadership Training — training Christian leaders — call for current classes.

6:00 PM *Featuring* The Issachar Report — Where Pastor Scheidbach addresses issues of concern to God fearing patriots, helping us understand current events in the light of God's Word.

We gather for public worship On Wednesday

7:00 PM *Featuring* prayer and Bible Preaching.

Radio/Podcast/YouTUBE Ministry: 12:00 PM Saturday, and 7 AM Sunday: KUHL 1440, podcast: brainmassage. net

www.santamarialighthouse.org

"God bless you! God bless America! and I'll See you in Church."

~ Index ~

~ Index ~

~ Index ~

K

L

M

N

O

P

R

~ Index ~

~ Index ~

~ Index ~

~ Index ~

JERRY SCHEIDBACH

HERMENEUTICS

Biblical
Principles of
Interpretation

THE
NEW CART
CHURCH

Doing the Right Thing the Wrong Way

Jerry Scheidbach

http://baptistlighthouse.org/bookstore/

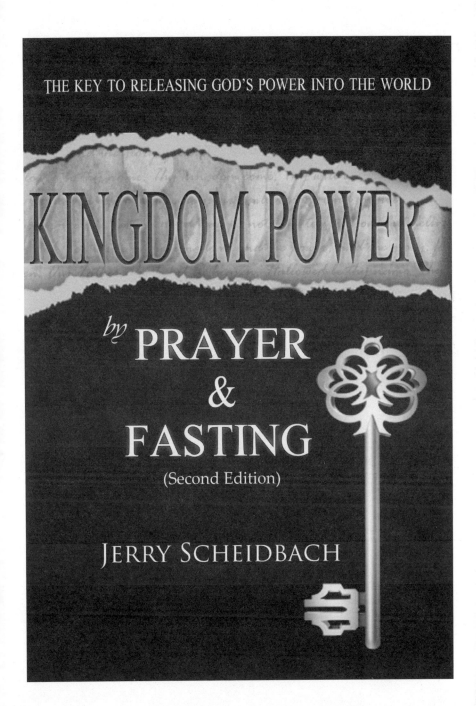

THE KEY TO RELEASING GOD'S POWER INTO THE WORLD

KINGDOM POWER

by PRAYER
&
FASTING

(Second Edition)

JERRY SCHEIDBACH

∽ My Notes On ∾

❧ The Visions of Daniel ☙

S C H E I D B A C H